Praise for Seth Kahan

"Seth lives and br[eathes] by example and s[hows] growth and beau[ty in] the practical elem[ents that] benefit from commu[nity]."

Susan Newman, Secretary General, International Real Estate Federation – USA

"Seth Kahan has a unique ability to entice us into building a community among association executives. He has been the inspirational and guiding force behind the CEO Community I belong to. He has done an excellent job of engaging us."

Mark G. Doherty, CAE, Executive Director of the Institute for Operations Research and the Management Sciences

"Seth brings an extraordinary level of passion, energy and spirit to the art of storytelling and the work of building community. His unique style at once challenges the intellect and soothes the soul."

Jeff De Cagna, Chief Strategist and Founder, Principled Innovation LLC and Association Community Thought Leader

"Seth brings the magic. If you follow his designs, you find it happening for you. His instructions and designs are clear and effective."

Madelyn Blair, CEO, Pelerei Inc.

"Seth Kahan's unique contribution has been to pioneer community-building within the institution helping to change the environment and make everyone feel part of it."

Gerry Rice, Internal Communications Director, The World Bank

"Having worked with Seth through the early days of the knowledge sharing program at the World Bank, I can attest to his abilities to build communities of practice. Seth creates an atmosphere of intimacy and involvement, whether the groups be small or large, 10 or 500+ people."

Lesley Shneier, Sr. Knowledge and Learning Specialist, The World Bank

BUILDING BEEHIVES

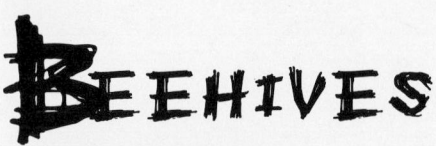

A **Handbook** for
Creating Communities
that **Generate Returns**

Seth Kahan
Organizational Community Specialist

© 2004 Seth Kahan

This book is copyrighted material. All rights reserved. It is against the law to make copies of this material without securing specific, written permission in advance from Seth Kahan.
Seth Kahan
P.O. Box 380
Glen Echo, Maryland 20812
U.S.A.
Seth@SethKahan.com
(301) 229-2221

No part of this publication may be reproduced, stored in retrieval systems, or transmitted in any form or by any means—including but not limited to electronic, mechanical, photocopying, and recording—without the prior written permission of the copyright holder.

Printed in the United States of America
Published by Performance Development Group, Inc.
Cover image by East of Beautiful, www.eastofbeautiful.com
Graphic design by Patricia Hord Graphik Design, www.phgd.com
ISBN 0-9759206-0-X

TABLE OF CONTENTS

v

Foreword by Susan Sarfati — vii

Introduction
Building Beehives: The Strategic
   Advantage of the Future — xi

The Sweet Rewards
Benefits of Building Beehives — 16
Three Ingredients for Heavenly Honey — 17
Case Study: The World Bank — 18

Bees at Work
Four Keys to Healthy Hives — 20
Ten Techniques for Building Beehives — 22

Making Meetings Hum
Cultivating Buzz — 28
Case Study: INFORMS — 30
Ten Techniques to Turn a
   Meeting into a Beehive — 32
Case Study: SIGMA — 40

The Language of the Hive
Storytelling – A Powerful Technique — 44
Case Study: Federal Chief
   Information Officers — 46
JumpStart Storytelling™ — 50

Conclusion — 53
Bibliography — 54
Acknowledgements — 56

How doth the little busy bee
Improve each shining hour,
And gather honey all day
From every opening flower!
—Isaac Watts' *Divine Songs*

FOREWORD

by Susan Sarfati

PRESIDENT & CEO, the Center for Association Leadership
Executive Vice President, American Society of Association Executives

The Center for Association Leadership is the primary learning and knowledge source for the association community. We are responsible for educational programs and events, future-focused research, knowledge resources, the building of learning communities and identifying and showcasing new ideas and thought-leaders relevant to association management and leadership.

We initiated our Center Visionary Program to recognize bold thinkers who were successfully implementing powerful, new ideas. We look for individuals who are at the forefront of change and will significantly impact the association community and society at large. In our first year we considered 24 exceptional nominees including business leaders, academics, writers and artists. We identified emerging thought leaders who we believe will have significant long-term influence on the thinking of the business and non-profit communities. In 2001, our inaugural year, we selected Seth Kahan to serve as one of our first Center Visionaries.

Without question Seth's work in organizational community, social capital, knowledge management and storytelling made him a stand out. Seth is a business revolutionary, stretching the limits of traditional thinking. His innovations have been successful in world-class organizations, such as the World Bank. There he successfully pioneered community-building in a multi-cultural, global environment.

Seth works closely with our staff, collaborates on the development of products and services, and writes extensively for our magazine. He can be counted on to develop unorthodox business solutions that demonstrate a deep concern for humanity. I often invite Seth to speak at meetings. He enlivens the room with his inspirational style, entertaining presentations and thought-provoking content.

I am pleased to introduce Building Beehives, *A Handbook for Creating Communities that Generate Returns*. It will help leaders in the association industry benefit from the strategic advantage of organizational community-building. Seth has successfully identified this emerging trend. He provides the information and techniques you need to put it to use, bringing new life, enthusiasm and value into your workplace. This handbook will help you harvest the sweet rewards that vibrant communities deliver.

Susan Sarfati
President & CEO
The Center for Association Leadership
Executive Vice President
American Society of Association Executives

"The future is already here —it's just unevenly distributed."

—William Gibson

で

INTRODUCTION

Building Beehives
The Strategic Advantage of the Future

It's hard to imagine the future. Yet, if we could, our strategic advantage would be enormous, setting us up to reach and exceed our dreams.

In 1992 it would have been difficult to imagine the Internet as a pervasive resource and business tool. Consider your response if someone had said to you, "You will have access to the sum total of human knowledge, at your fingertips, 24 hours a day, 365 days a year. You will be able to teach yourself accounting, how to repair a computer, or the history of space exploration at 3 am on New Year's eve if you're motivated... and so will everyone else."

Those who understood what was coming positioned themselves to win big:
- Yahoo!—First to make it really easy to find sites on the web
- Cisco—Provider of the cables & computers that built the web
- University of Phoenix Online—Helping people earn degrees over the web

What radical innovation is today emerging that can be used for strategic advantage?

Imagine this... a new kind of community in which people work together with colleagues, stakeholders, business partners... and in some cases, even competitors... to share what they know and achieve results that are far beyond what any one can accomplish alone. The learning takes place in real time, drawing on all levels of experience to take performance and output to extraordinary new levels.

Organizations around the world have been studying just how to do this for decades, with major advances in the last ten years. We are learning how to bring people together and turn them into learning-communities that accelerate performance. I call these unique groups, *beehives*.

In your imagination, envision a buzzing hive. Hear the hum. Feel the vibration of bees at work. No one is in charge—not even the queen bee.
Research shows she does not direct the workers. In fact, each bee "knows" what to do. They carry out their cooperative tasks based on cues they receive from each other and the environment. Yet, they work together as if guided by a greater intelligence. Together, their efforts cascade into the wisdom of the hive. They are building honeycomb, lining it with sweet rewards at speeds that defy the imagination.

What a wonder it is to see a project team, a meeting, a committee or a group of volunteers turn into a beehive. The transformation can be startling. One moment they are all over the map, moving in random fashion, blocking each other and coming up with off-the-wall ideas that go in different directions. Then, in a turn of events, as if a hidden conductor stepped in, the group gels into a highly coordinated collaboration. The results are marvelous. People compliment each other in their approaches, playing off each other's strengths and supporting each other's weaknesses like a champion sports team.

Much work has been done in recent years to study how people work and learn together. Research on collaboration and social learning has spawned experiments in many organizations. This handbook is the result of my experience with some of those companies.

Equally, there have been great strides in collaborative technologies. However, I steer clear of them in this handbook. I have seen communities form with no more technology than a three-ring binder, and I have worked on some of the most advanced Knowledge Management Systems being developed. My focus in this brief handbook is to give you tools from improving human interaction, regardless of the technology in use.

In the World Bank I helped establish the successful knowledge management initiative that began in 1996. Communities (called *thematic groups*) were named the "heart and soul" of the effort. They were recognized to be the source of group learning and know-how, where professionals shared their experience and applied it to new situations.

I participated in think-tanks that included diverse industries and academia, all interested in the power of communities to develop and apply knowledge. Included were professionals from Harvard, MicroSoft, Intel, Buckman Laboratories, IBM, Disney, Defense Information Systems Agency, U.S. Army, U.S. Navy, Ernst and Young, Lucent Technologies, Johns Hopkins University, and the American Productivity and Quality Center.

In 2001 after I received the Visionary award from the Center for Association Leadership I began to work with associations. Community is a core competency in the association world, where member benefits join the bottom line in priority. Meetings, conferences and conventions, play a critical role for every association, providing learning and networking opportunities for members and often serving as a primary source of revenue.

Together with executives from diverse associations I have explored the uses of community to generate returns. These included those that were large and small, professional and trade, local and global. CEOs and senior staff from the American College of Cardiology, Project Management Institute, Center for American Nurses, the Fulbright Association, the Society of Independent Gasoline Marketers of America, the Institute for Operations Research and the Management Sciences, the International Real Estate Federation, the Urban Land Institute, and the American Society of Association Executives and others have been involved.

Community is how people have always worked and learned together. For thousands of years we have depended on communities for survival. Modern research is showing that our unique capacity to learn was made possible through our relationships to our families, our tribes, our villages. Your presence here today, as you read this handbook, is a testimony to the success of our ancestors' communities to deliver on the bottom line: survival.

Times have changed, but community continues to give us the upper hand. We use technology to reach around the world and bring the best minds available together in virtual communities. We cross organizational boundaries, bringing together senior managers and workers to collaborate. Communities grow outside the organization when business partners, stakeholders, members and employees come together to develop new solutions to tough problems. They are in coffee shops, living rooms, hallways and board rooms... Beehives are *everywhere.*

But, most organizations today do not make use of community. They rely on traditional management alone to get work done. They are like those in the early 90s who didn't understand the Internet and plodded along thinking it to be a fad that would come and go.

This is why building beehives can be a strategic advantage. Embrace this way of working and learning together, and you will move out in front. You will harness the power of collective wisdom, leading the way into the next generation of professional development and innovation.

In this handbook I have put the tools and techniques I use to create organizational communities which generate returns. I hope you will put them into practice. Because if you do, the rewards will be sweet!

Seth Kahan
Seth@SethKahan.com

THE SWEET REWARDS

Beehives make **HONEY.** This means they achieve **RETURNS.**

Benefits of Building Beehives

For the beekeeper (the organization):

- Better project execution
- Faster training through sharing of on-the-job know-how
- Higher employee and member satisfaction
- Effective innovation
- More informed decision-making
- Improved communications and coordination
- Greater acceptance of new products and services
- Stronger partnerships

For the bees (the people who participate):

- Higher trust and confidence
- Increased learning
- Higher visibility
- Professional development
- Performance improvement
- Better access to experts and resources
- Greater awareness of colleagues' activities
- Benefit of others' points-of-view

Three Ingredients for Heavenly Honey

For a beehive to generate good returns, three forces must be optimized: business benefits, community concerns and participant payoffs. Each must be thoughtfully, clearly articulated and properly supported to ensure your beehives are making the best honey possible.

1. Business Benefits—Why does a beekeeper build beehives? For honey. Before you decide to build with your time and money, put your eye on the returns. Examples of business benefits:
- Increases in membership
- Improved communications
- Better product and services development
- Improved operational performance
- Increased skill for staff members

2. Community Concerns—These are the common causes that unite the members, causing the community to form. This is what turns a group of bees into a hive. Community concerns are the shared motivation that drives people to collaborate and make contributions. These concerns must compliment the business drivers.
Examples of community concerns:
- Championing a social cause
- Executing a complex task
- Contributing to a field of expertise
- Receiving group recognition or advancement
- Achieving political objectives

3. Participant Payoffs—This is what motivates each person to show up and give their best. Since beehives are a volunteer activity, the payoff must be clear and inspiring.
Examples of participant payoffs
- Skill building
- Receiving recognition
- Achieving proximity to power
- Obtaining professional advancement
- Gaining access to peers for problem-solving

Case Study: World Bank

In 2002 at the World Bank I worked with President James Wolfensohn. My task was to build internal communities that would help him accomplish strategic objectives and improve communications.

The World Bank's mission is to alleviate poverty. Wolfensohn spoke forcefully about the need to create partnerships with the poor to accomplish this. However, I observed that this initiative seemed to lack the traction it deserved inside the organization.

I began to assemble a group to help him address the issue. I didn't have far to look. In the front window of the World Bank bookstore was the book, *Voices of the Poor*[1]. I contacted one of the editors and within a few weeks we had arranged a coffee between Wolfensohn and twenty staff members who had been studying the complex topic of working in partnership with the poor. Our beehive was beginning to form.

The first get-together was abuzz with conversation and ideas. There were a series of further coffees followed by papers and soon Wolfensohn was incorporating ideas from this group in his conversations with heads of state around the world. At the same time, news of the collaboration was spreading among those staff concerned with the issue, pulling more in to help.

This beehive only lasted a few short months, but the work it did was significant. Let's take a look at the business benefits, community concerns and participant payoffs that made this beehive a success.

Business Benefits:
- Strategy development on core objective: Empowering the Poor
- Improved internal communications

Community Concerns:
- Championing the cause of Empowering the Poor
- Group recognition for those working on this topic

Personal Payoffs:
- Receiving recognition for professional contribution
- Achieving proximity to power, audience with the president
- Using professional expertise to make a difference in the world

[1] Narayan, Deepa (editor) and Walton, Michael (editor), *Voices of the Poor: From Many Lands*, World Bank Publications, 2002

BEES AT WORK

Community is
the **heart** and **soul** of
professionals
working together

Four Keys to Healthy Hives

Imagine…

- A tightly knit group of champions meets every Monday morning to update each other and surface issues as they **role out a complex** change initiative. Together they **identify common problems, develop solutions they will coordinate across the organization,** and provide each other with **personal and professional support.**

- Communication constituencies meet with the CEO and Senior Management Team at biweekly coffees. In a relaxed atmosphere they share tasty desserts and brainstorm how **strategic objectives can gain better traction internally.** When they go back to their offices they talk about their visit "upstairs," batting around ideas with the president. The follow-up conversations with colleagues bring important insights that feed the next coffee with the CEO and **spread news organically.**

- In the cafeteria every month technical experts have lunch together and troubleshoot problems that are cropping up in the cracks between their departments. Together they identify issues, **generate grass roots solutions**, sidestep bureaucracy and **keep their projects on the fast track.**

Each of these is a beehive… these groups are highly motivated to work toward goals that benefit organizational performance. What makes them function at their best? Here are four keys to optimize the health of hives.

1. Keep membership voluntary.

When people volunteer, they choose to get involved only if the rewards are personal. This type of motivation is different from responding to a mandate. In this case, they are choosing to invest their time, attention and efforts because it will help them to achieve more than they could alone.

2. **Let beehives be autonomous, operate outside traditional bureaucracy.**
   Although they receive sponsorship from the organization, activities are not bound by traditional command-and-control decision-making. This gives the beehive flexibility and freedom which is one of its advantages. Where will decision-making come from, if not through traditional management?
   The process is developed within the beehive, shaped by the members based on their best judgment. In some beehives a new, smaller version of command-and-control will emerge. In others there will be varieties of democratic coordination. It is important that you allow the control structure to emerge from the members. If it is imposed from outside, you will not have a beehive.

3. **Allow beehives to be driven by members' common concerns.**
   Community achieves its power when it enables members to act on their common concerns. As they contribute together, they turn competition on its head. Contribution is a fundamentally different approach to getting work done than exists in most organizations. It accentuates successful accomplishment of the group's goals rather than individual achievement. To do this well the group must cultivate individual talent as well as collective capacity. This is real synergy... and it comes from giving people the opportunity to work on what they truly care about.

4. **Let beehives grow ecologically.** Operating outside the organizational chart, beehives are free to cross boundaries. They may confer new status on people, making new types of collaboration possible. They may engage those who have not been included in the past.

These keys may seem counter-intuitive, as if they will create clashes with management. In fact, beehives are powerful because they operate outside the organizational chart. This makes them a wonderful compliment to hierarchy. Traditional management and beehives enhance each other; where one is weak, the other is strong.

Ten Techniques for Building Beehives

Building beehives requires a new way of looking at the world. The main task of management, when working with a community, changes from supervising sub-ordinates to enabling colleagues. People, in their hearts and minds, hold the perspectives, the knowledge and the experience that will create the honey in the hive.

To bring this know-how to bear on organizational needs, managers need to cultivate relationships built on trust and healthy growth. Here are ten techniques that embrace this new way of working, giving guidance on how to build beehives that deliver results.

1. Share the idea of your beehive with everyone who has a stake its success.
This includes those who will gain from the business benefits being achieved, such as managers, members, clients and stakeholders. Also include those who support the community's concerns. This may bring you into contact with people outside your normal sphere of influence, such as members of academia, research groups and policy organizations. Each of these people has the potential to make valuable contributions to your community and help your organization achieve its goals.

2. Interact with potential bees.
Talk with people. Ask for ideas, suggestions, and the names of others who would benefit by taking part. Listen to their perspective, especially if different from your own. You may be able to identify new participant payoffs. Embrace multiple perspectives as long as everyone is working toward the same concerns.

3. Identify a coordinator

This is one of the two most important roles in the beehive.
Responsibilities include:
- Identifying important issues as they arise
- Planning and facilitation of events
- Linking members of the beehive
- Fostering professional development
- Coordinating development of documents, websites, learning events
- Cultivating the health of the beehive

This should be a "people person" with strong interpersonal communication skills and a genuine desire to help the community succeed.

4. Identify resident experts.

This is the second most important role in your beehive. These people will have "deep" knowledge of the community concerns. For example, if your beehive focuses on how to improve the annual meeting, the resident experts will have knowledge of the annual meeting in all of its varying capacities (history, revenue source, vendors & exhibitors, membership, professional contributions, etc.). The resident experts are sources of guidance for group decisions. They wield their authority through their know-how and experience, rather than by decree.

5. Invite people to participate.

Communicate to people through their preferred media. If they are telephone people, call them. If they are email people, write them. If they read Discovery Magazine, put an ad in it. In your invitation, be clear about (a) the business benefits, (b) the community concerns and (c) the participant payoffs. Tell them what you are hoping to accomplish and ask them to be part of the effort

6. Make it easy for members to contact each other.

As soon as the beehive forms, publish a directory with phone numbers, email addresses, and expertise. You may wish to include a section in the directory which members fill in any way they want. If they choose to put in personal information (e.g., "I like to sail and have three grandkids"), it will help increase rapport with colleagues. If they choose to put in requests for assistance (e.g., "I need help increasing membership"), it facilitates transactions within the community.

7. Invite open discussions.

Allow divergent ideas; don't push consensus. If small groups form in your community to champion an alternative perspective, help them explore further. This multiplicity of perspective bolsters the work. Tackling issues from many sides is one of the strengths of a community. As long as people are focused on the same shared concerns of the group, differing perspectives strengthen their abilities.

8. Communicate, Communicate, And Communicate!

Do everything you can to keep people in the loop. Come to know your beehive's preferred communication vehicles and use them. There will probably be several. You may need brownbag lunches, one-on-one meetings among core members, emails and listservs. Do whatever works. It is no accident that the words **communication** and **community** have the same root. Whenever possible have beehive members take responsibility for the communication. Construct communiqués so that they invite participation (e.g., rather than exhaustive minutes, highlight main points & invite others to fill in gaps).

9. Stay open to continued suggestions

The community will evolve. This is normal. A community is a living thing and changes over time. Create ways for new ideas to be reviewed and processed easily without derailing progress.

10. Develop presentation toolkits

Make it easy for members of the beehive to share their work with colleagues and other interested people. You may wish to assist them in developing PowerPoint presentations, brochures, CDs, or product samples. These toolkits support your beehive's success. Each member will reach into other communities to support and endorse the work they are doing in this beehive. Toolkits make that easier.

TEN Techniques for Building Beehives

1. **Share the idea** of your beehive with everyone who has a stake in its success.

2. **Interact** with potential bees.

3. Identify a **coordinator**

4. Identify **resident experts**.

5. **Invite people** to participate.

6. **Make it easy** for the members to contact each other.

7. Invite **open discussions.**

8. **Communicate, Communicate,** And **Communicate!**

9. **Stay open** to continued suggestions

10. Develop **presentation toolkits**

MAKING MEETINGS HUM

From the participant's perspective, community is what takes a meeting beyond the ordinary and makes it both an extraordinary experience and a cherished memory.

Cultivating Buzz

When a meeting begins to buzz, it is something to treasure. People work together in an *esprit de corps* that enhances each person's contribution. The group achieves more than the sum of its participants. It becomes easier for everyone to get what they came for.

People initiate professional relationships, increase their know-how and expertise, find job opportunities, let others know about their offerings, and have more fun. Every meeting coordinator hopes for the magical moment when their event transforms into a memorable gathering that takes on a spirit of its own and really begins to buzz.

Not all meetings achieve this. Some will say, 'That doesn't happen here. We don't do the Kum-Ba-Ya thing.' They mistakenly think of community as holding hands and hugging. But, this is a limited view of the power of people to collaborate. Community enhances the most professional meetings, especially those dealing with demanding topics.

In the context of a meeting, a beehive is a group of people working together and sharing what they know to serve a common set of concerns. It is a superior form of collaboration with three important aspects.

- **Working together** can take many forms. It can be done virtually, over the web or it can be face-to-face. Either way people choose to co-create because they know they can accomplish more together than separately.
- **Sharing know-how and experience,** learning together, is the heart of community. It happens when everyone involved joins in the spirit of collaboration.
- **Common concerns** are what brings it all together: caring. This form of attention combines sensitivity with a personal stake in achieving the group's goals.

Anytime these three emerge, you have a powerhouse that cannot be beat. Bring them out in a meeting and you have an experience that will propel your group into new levels of excellence and create memories.

Community cannot be mandated. If the boss walks in and demands, "Everybody collaborate!" it is less likely that a community will form. However, the good news is that a beehive can be deliberately cultivated. Community is a quality that exists in all groups of people. Under the right circumstances it will emerge. The way to bring it out is by putting the right conditions in place and rewarding its appearance when it shows. It is an organic rather than a mechanical process. You cannot command a beehive into existence, but you can grow one.

Case Study: INFORMS[1]

Mark G. Doherty, CAE, and Executive Director of the Institute for Operations Research and the Management Sciences (INFORMS) uses community building to generate income and provide value to his members by cultivating a business model that thrives on social and intellectual capital.

INFORMS has 11,000 members that include scientists, students, educators, managers and business professionals. Two thirds of the annual budget comes from subscriptions of the 12 publications it produces. These periodicals are respected by professional and academic circles in their fields. In total, INFORMS publishes almost 1,000 articles, 10,000 pages, and 58 issues per year. Another quarter of INFORMS' annual budget comes from its meetings. These two pillars—publications and meetings—support a very successful business model.

"There are two things we are about: social capital as demonstrated by our meetings and the intellectual capital which we document through our publications," says Doherty. "The two are intrinsically linked." Social capital can be defined as human relationships and interactions that generate value, including revenue. Intellectual capital can be thought of as knowledge used to create income. Doherty understands both and combines them, creating a powerful symbiosis.

INFORMS hosts three meetings per year. One is a new-practice conference. People come to hear experts in the field discuss the latest and the greatest. The other two meetings provide a forum for the development of new ideas, providing almost every participant with the opportunity to share what they are learning.

Of 3,000 who attend the annual meeting, as many as 2,400 may present. There are often 50 concurrent sessions. Doherty says, "It is a very exciting place to be. There are intellectual debates, disagreements, multi-university collaborations, cross-pollination of ideas. It's a meeting people love to attend. Repeats are astonishingly high. It's their opportunity to gather with colleagues, hear about the new-fangled things that are going on. We focus on new or soon-to-be minted Ph.D.s and will soon include the same for masters' degrees. Students get involved at an early age. This is social capital at its best."

The meetings result in more than 5,000 articles submitted for publication to INFORMS every year. The quality of these submissions makes it possible for the highly prized journals to publish papers that represent the best in the field, securing their niche as leading periodicals. Several INFORMS journals are tracked by the *Financial Times* and *BusinessWeek*, among others, as indicators for trends in intellectual capital.

Doherty's success is founded on his understanding of how to successfully combine interaction at meetings with the publication of his periodicals. He brings his members together in professionally stimulating environments that generate new ideas. Then he harvests the resulting knowledge. The journals provide members with recognition in their field, while at the same time documenting the best of their contributions.

Doherty remarks, "We have hit the bull's eye by realizing how important social capital is to the dynamics of our organization. Bringing our people together in ways that stimulate their collaboration is how we use community to generate a continuous stream of knowledge that we can document and sell. At the same time, we are providing our members with the best opportunity in their field to interact and grow. It's a win for us all."

[1] First published by Executive Update, March 2004 as *Community Business Models: Spotlight on INFORMS*

TEN Techniques to Turn a Meeting into a Beehive

1. Let every participant know they are valued.
2. Include social events as part of the agenda.
3. Shift general sessions to business-casual
4. Designate a "Conference Weaver"
5. Create opportunities for people to speak to the plenary.
6. Provide ice breakers.
7. Get speakers involved.
8. Get organizational leaders & membership involved.
9. Give participants the chance to reflect together.
10. Highlight magic moments.

In my experience working in conferences of all sizes, from less than a hundred to several thousands, building a beehive is always possible. Whether people attend from many countries or one, the potential is alive. Blue collar workers, white collar professionals, young and old... we all want to be part of an event that buzzes. Let's take a look at ten techniques to turn your next meeting into a beehive.

1. Let every participant know they are valued.
People must be treated with respect to come out of their shells. Make it known to each person that they are welcome at the event. This can be as simple as

making sure there is a registration packet for them when they arrive to providing individuals with a concierge who will help them network and make professional connections. Letting your participants know they are welcome guests will set you up for success. Here are ideas for bringing this to life:

- Ensure that conference materials, including nametags, are prepared and waiting. You may wish to include other forms of recognition with the registration materials including gifts. The more personalized the better.
- Hold receptions in which participants are sought out and recognized for their professional contributions, especially if they have demonstrated support of your goals.
- Take guests' concerns seriously. When participants make the effort to seek you out and share their thoughts, listen to them and follow up thoughtfully.
- Find out what your attendees want to accomplish when they attend. By acting as a facilitator, assisting them in achieving their objectives you not only build good will with the participants, but you gain access to important market knowledge. Understand why people attend your meetings and you have knowledge that can be used to improve their experience, draw their colleagues, and grow your meeting attendance.

2. Include social events as part of the agenda.

All meetings benefit by providing participants with opportunities to interact in gracious and accommodating formats. Some of the most important transactions take place over meals, coffee, and in the presence of entertainment. When you design a gathering to include cordial times for coming together, you set the stage for an added dimension of interaction. Savvy conference goers will see this opportunity for what it is: a chance to meet others outside formal proceedings. Ideas include:

- Find ways for people to mix and talk seamlessly. For example, you might arrange stations in which food is prepared in entertaining ways, so that people can gather and chat as they watch.

- Include enough structure at your social events to allow people to meet new faces, but not so much that it constrains the interactions. You may include an ice-breaker such as an entertainer who involves the audience, but keep the performance short so there is plenty of time for people to chat and move about on their own.
- Whenever possible, have events that are open to all participants. You want to build a broad feeling of inclusion, and this is an easy way to open the doors.
- Design "off-time" including time prior to the meeting, coffee breaks and post-meeting interactions. Make it easy for people to mix and mingle in informal ways. Critical transactions often take place during these "breaks" in the program.

3. Shift general sessions to business-casual

Business-casual beats formal attire every time for helping people relax and participate. I have seen over-dress kill the social potential of a gathering by stiffening the interactions. Yet casual is too loose. In today's world combining serious intentions (business) with informal rapport (casual) is the magic combination for bringing people together. General session techniques which compliment business-casual include:

- Choose event locations where the chairs are movable rather than nailed to the floor and position them so that they arc around the speaking platform, rather than face front in militaristic rows.
- Add living room decor where possible, such as flowers and plants, coffee tables and water glasses.
- Rather than having microphones stationed so that people have to walk to them and stand in line, have wireless microphones and microphone "runners," people who are assigned to bring the microphones to participants. When possible allow the participants to hand the microphones back and forth to each other, as the microphone runners step aside. Passing the microphone back and forth is an often overlooked way for people to begin to interact with each other. It works especially well as a simple ice-breaker in a stiff crowd.

4. Designate a "Conference Weaver"
Many meetings are now incorporating this new role. A conference weaver is a person who takes responsibility for seeing that participants are engaged and their needs are met. Sometimes he or she will act as emcee, literally weaving together the different presentations and highlighting how each contributes to the overall program goals. The conference weaver provides whatever it takes to jumpstart the conference and keep energy high. This can include inspirational sound bytes, logistical coordination and *ad hoc* facilitation. Here are ways a conference weaver can contribute:

- Anytime the plenary is not in session, they meet one-on-one with several participants. In these private interactions they take the temperature on how the conference is going by asking questions like:
    - How is it going for you?
    - Is there anything that would improve the meeting?
    - Is there anyone you would like to meet?
- Regular meetings with the conference coordinators are opportune moments for the weaver to communicate what they have been learning from participants. Whenever a change is made based on participant requests, it should be communicated to the plenary. This makes participants feel more ownership of the event.
- When participants request sessions that have not been programmed (but fit inside the conference goals), the weaver can be available to improvise and meet their needs.

5. Create opportunities for people to speak to the plenary.
Speaking to the plenary is extremely valuable to participants, providing visibility, increasing everyone's ability to network, and establishing a sense of ownership for participants. These sessions can be short (as little as twenty seconds per person) or longer, designed as significant portions of the program agenda. They should be focused on the business at hand to ensure continuity. Here are suggestions for how to make this happen:

- For best results, repeat short sessions of introductions throughout the conference. For example, three minutes in the morning, three minutes

- at lunch and five minutes at the close of the day. For big conferences, add opportunities for participants to speak during the breakout sessions.
- To increase participation—especially useful when luminaries attend—design a presentation around the attendees and their contributions to the field. Have a moderator who recognizes selected participants and facilitates their interaction with the plenary.
- Contact new participants—and others you wish to welcome— in advance and ask them to say a couple of words to the larger group. Let them know how much time they will have and give them tips on how to keep their comments relevant.
- Establish a theme and invite people to share their perspective at various points in the meeting. This allows them to introduce themselves to the others at the meeting while making a substantive contribution.

6. Provide ice breakers.

These activities add to the fun and make it easy for participants to increase rapport with their colleagues. For example, include in the speakers' introductions a personal fact related to the theme of the conference. At an Innovation convention, each speaker could share their favorite invention. A game could be added in which participants match names of inventors with their invention. These simple devices give people conversation starters that are consistent with the goals of the meeting. Here are ideas:

- Ask people to share with a neighbor what they hope to get out of the conference, or name one objective they have in attending. This can be done even in large groups of several thousand. When the room fills with the buzz of everyone talking, it creates a highly stimulating environment.
- Give people a task that meshes with the meeting agenda and folds nicely into a facilitated discussion you have planned. Prompt them with both an easy question as well as a provocative one. This makes it easy for everyone to participate.
- Consider sharing the ice breaker in advance with those you can count on to participate and invite them to make a particularly stimulating contribution in the plenary.

7. Get speakers involved.

Speakers are the role models of meetings. With minor changes, adding a sentence or two to their presentation, they can catapult your conference to a new level. Ask every speaker to endorse the building of your meeting's community by encouraging people to meet each other. Here are ways they can contribute:

- Ask speakers to recognize those who have a particular capacity to contribute because of their unique experience. Have the speakers invite participants to approach these VIP attendees with questions.
- Following a presentation, have your speakers interact with participants in an informal setting. Here they can be effective at starting important conversations. This works especially well for those that require finesse, such as controversial topics.
- Speakers carry celebrity status and can be used to leverage your conference goals. Give your speakers assignments based on your objectives.
- Request that your speakers give "homework," asking participants to initiate topical discussions during the breaks.
- Invite speakers to model the behaviors you have requested of your participants. For example, if you have asked people share their objectives for the meeting, have the speaker begin by sharing his or her objectives.

8. Get organizational leaders and staff members involved.

Everyone likes to know that the "home team" is present and engaged. It comforts and engages the audience. When employees of the sponsoring organization take the time to reach out, people always see it as a sign of graciousness. Here are some ways to do this:

- Executives, board members and employees can work the room, introducing themselves and helping participants feel welcome. They are the authorities at the meeting. Their support and personal welcome means a great deal to attendees and will boost enthusiasm. This helps to create a positive, upbeat atmosphere.
- Staff members can provide needed assistance to meeting attendees, helping them with everything from getting a chair to acting as a concierge. This support creates the social infrastructure that enables people to relax and get involved.

9. Give participants the chance to reflect together.
Time can be set aside during the meeting in which people reflect together in large or small groups. Reflection is a critical part of the learning process that is often overlooked. Many conference planners want to pack in as much information as possible, so that participants will feel that they are getting what they paid for. A short reflective experience provides the necessary leverage to turn this information into useful applications, or "takeaways," for the participants. Here are ideas to consider:

- Hold a general session in which people are asked to develop ideas that make substantive contributions to the meeting's goals. With a trained facilitator who knows how to draw people out and nurture a conversation, this can quickly turn into high-performance collaboration.
- Invite participants of breakout sessions to work together and address controversial topics. Then report the highpoints of their debates to the plenary or post them where they can be reviewed by everybody.
- Bring in an innovator, someone with an outside perspective, and use their presentation to stimulate out-of-the-box thinking. Take time for attendees to draw links between the innovative content and the conference program.
- Design a session in which people are given concrete ways to contribute to the overall success of the meeting. For example, I once asked participants to write down their ideas for the future of the profession. These were collected, typed up and distributed the following day when they were used as the basis for a presentation.

10. Highlight magic moments.
This is perhaps most important. When a powerful moment transpires, be prepared to draw everyone's attention to it. If your meeting is well-programmed, it is easy to be carried along by the pace and run right over a noteworthy incident. Yet, this is a golden opportunity for transformation and should not be overlooked. Here are thoughts on how to highlight these special occasions without losing momentum:

- Program an extra fifteen minutes of "buffer time" in each day. When a magic moment occurs, take a pause. Praise the moment as the type of experience that makes this meeting special.

- Acknowledge efforts by participants which go the extra mile. Reward people for taking initiative and creating something extraordinary
- Have enough flexibility in the program that you can literally redesign a portion of your agenda based on the participants' needs. There is no better way to show that their experience is the most important part of your meeting.
- Interview participants and locate those that have done something special in the preceding year. Give them time in the program to say a little about their work and incorporate some response from the audience.
- Be on the lookout for exceptional moments in the meeting. Whenever one occurs ask yourself how it can be leveraged to take the results of the conference to a new level. By looking for opportunities to raise the bar on performance and building in the necessary flexibility, you set yourself up for success.

Community is always an added value. Consider your participants' experience. From the individual's perspective, being inside a beehive is what takes a meeting beyond the ordinary into the extraordinary.

Case Study: SIGMA[1]

Making community work meeting after meeting, year after year requires an approach that overarches and informs every activity. It requires attention to the details that make or break each event. Ken Doyle, executive vice president of the Society of Independent Gasoline Marketers of America (SIGMA) has been building the community of SIGMA's members since 1980.

Members of SIGMA own chains of gasoline stations and other distribution systems that buy motor fuel from manufacturers and sell it to end consumers. SIGMA membership ranges from individuals who own ten gasoline stations in rural America to 7-Eleven, with 37,000 gasoline stations. On average, SIGMA members sell more than 200 million gallons a year, and together, all members sell 57 billion gallons of motor fuel a year.

Human interaction at meetings is central to Doyle's philosophy. He says, "It's all social networking. There's an expectation when you go to a SIGMA meeting that you're going to have an opportunity to meet with your fellow wizards—other people who do the same thing you do but with whom you don't compete. Everything we do at our conventions is geared toward providing an opportunity for our members to interact."

Doyle came to this philosophy from his experience in college as social chairman in a fraternity house. "I realized having a good party was really important. If everybody had a good time, it was great; if people had a bad time, they told you about it for weeks! I have to laugh, because you know in a fraternity house, you have the same group of guys, and you have one party one week and it's absolutely fabulous. Everyone is up dancing and talking about what a fabulous time they had. And the next week you have the same party, the same people, the same group, the same band, the same everything, and it's a real snoozer. Everybody's gone by 10:30 and complaining all week. I got interested in how you create an environment where people have fun. When people have fun, they learn, and they want to come back and do it all over again."

SIGMA has three meetings per year, fall and spring conventions with attendance of about 600, and a winter management conference with 250-300 in attendance.

"On a typical day, we have a buffet breakfast. The room is set tight. There are no empty chairs. Everyone who comes in can stand in line and talk. They can go to the waffle machine and talk. They can go to the omelet station and talk. They can go to the coffee station and talk. They can sit at the table and talk. If you've been to three SIGMA meetings, you know everyone in the room when you walk in, and you know you will get to catch up with friends and meet new people.

"After breakfast we have a legislative meeting, a giant meeting in which all of our members have a chance to speak up on legislation. We talk about what the government is doing and what we need to do to comply. There is a real openness and a feeling that they are actually participating in making the decisions, because they are.

"At our spring convention, we have golf and we hand-select the pairings. We know who gets along and who doesn't get along. We know who not to put in a group. People call us up and say, 'You know, I'd really like to get to know so-and-so, can I get in his group?' We try to take care of that if we can. I've had more members come back to me and say, 'You know, I met so-and-so and we played golf. I never thought I'd do business with his company. Now we're doing 90 million gallons a year with them.'

"We work really hard for all the new people who come into SIGMA. Our staff introduces them around. We find fuel suppliers who are interested in their business; we fix them up. We find the people who are non-competitors but who are similar size and types of business. We give them big brothers. We get them involved on committees.

"I am always thinking about how we get people to talk. When there's a new issue in the industry, I begin asking myself, 'How do we get people talking about that?' Our members are at the cutting edge of their business. They're trying stuff that nobody else has ever done before. They learn from each other. Everything we do is just to get them there to sit around and talk. I sit there some mornings, watching them drink coffee together, and I am just amazed at the amount of business that I see getting done."

[1] First published by Executive Update, January 2004 as *Encouraging Community*

STORYTELLING: LANGUAGE OF THE HIVE

Storytelling—a Powerful Technique

If there is a language of engagement, it is storytelling. In recent years it has been increasingly recognized as a powerful business tool.

> *Time after time, when faced with the task of persuading a group of managers or front-line staff in a large organization to get enthusiastic about a major change… storytelling was the only thing that worked.*
> —Stephen Denning, former program director, The World Bank, and author[1]

Storytelling has the ability to change minds, move people emotionally and engage them deeply.

> *Transformation is the result of a well-told story.*
> —Society of Organizational Learning and Massachusetts Institute of Technology[2].

When people share their stories, they reveal much about their identity and their values as well as what they what they know.

> *Storytelling is increasingly seen as an important tool for communicating explicit and especially tacit knowledge—not just information but know-how*
> —Larry Prusak[3], Managing Principal of IBM Consulting Group with Don Cohen

Storytelling serves the building of beehives in three important ways:

1. **When people tell their stories, they join the group.**
   By telling a personal story the storyteller makes himself part of the community. When the story is done, the person who told the story *belongs*. By having every person in a group tell a story from their experience, you create a shared frame-of-reference that includes everyone in the room. There is no more effective way to start a beehive than with a good storytelling session.

2. **Mutual trust is increased between teller and listeners.**
   When people listen to someone tell their story, they get a sense of how her mind works and what is important to her. This is a powerful way to build the rapport required for working together productively.

3. Storytelling is how people share what they know.

A story can be thought of as the *smallest portable context*[4]. It does more than transport the listener. Embedding itself in his memory, the story attaches to all related information. This quality of association, it turns out, is incredibly valuable. Information out of context is at best transactional and at worse, misinformation. But, stories come with their own built-in circumstances. These situational nuances clarify, highlight, dramatize and accentuate. The resulting contexts assist the listener in understanding the information, and storing it so it can be recalled and re-applied in new situations.

---

[1] *The Springboard: How Storytelling Ignites Action in Knowledge-era Organization,* Butterworth Heinemann, 2000, and *Squirrel, Inc. – A Fable of Leadership through Storytelling,* Jossey-Bass, 2004
[2] *The Four Elements of Every Successful Story,* Society of Organizational Learning and Massachusetts Institute of Technology, Reflections, Volume 4, Number 3.
[3] *In Good Company, How Social Capital Makes Organizations Work,* Harvard Business School Press, 2001
[4] Interview of John Seely Brown, former Chief Scientist of Xerox Corporation and Director of the Palo Alto Research Center, by Seth Kahan conducted February, 2003. Transcript is available at www.SethKahan.com under Resources.

Case Study: Federal Chief Information Officers[1]

In 2000 a government group of chief information officers (CIOs) gathered to explore how organizations were building successful knowledge-sharing initiatives in cultures in which information hoarding, competitiveness, and secrecy were the norm. This group invited me to share how to build community in a business setting. I wanted to do more than talk about it. I wanted the CIOs to experience it.

I set the stage by telling my own story and inviting others to share their stories. This approach led to a blossoming of openness and collaboration that was remarkable.

I started with my story for two reasons. First, I have learned that *how we share* is equally important as what we share, so I like to start with a story I can tell in a relaxed and comfortable way. Second, I model the same vulnerability that I later ask of the participants by sharing a personal perspective, yet without going overboard into a "touchy-feely" session.

I spoke of the social transformation that is taking place in knowledge-sharing organizations. Many companies are bumbling along, trying to help staff move from a dependent, childlike relationship with the organization, to an adult relationship in which leadership is shared and meaningful contributions are possible. The murmurs and nodding of heads in my audience told me the CIOs could relate to this.

I then ask my audience to indulge me by listening to a poem that I often use. This poem is called the "Prayer of the Three Times.[2]" I told the CIOs that when I finished reciting the poem, I would ask them to share something about what they experienced as listeners. They shift in their seats, noticeably uncomfortable. I have seen this before and I reassure them that participation is entirely voluntary. I let them know any response is acceptable, including, "The poem did nothing for me," or "I didn't like the poem." All I asked was that they listen to the poem and be prepared to share their experience.

With this introduction, I pick up a Tibetan prayer gong, a small bowl that makes a wonderful sound when struck, and I asked them to listen quietly. Here is the poem:

Gonggg...

> If time was not an obstacle and we could invite all of our ancestors to be here, present with us, what would they tell us?
>
> If our grandparents... and their parents...could be here, what would they have to say about our work in the world? They would not be contained by the views we hold, by the constraints we place upon ourselves, by the politics of our workplace...

Gonggg...

> If time was not an obstacle and we could invite all of the children-yet-to-be-born here with us now, what would they tell us?
>
> Could they help us remember that the world we are building is the world they will inherit?

G o n g g g ...

> If space was not an obstacle and we could invite everyone in the world to be here, present with us now, what could we do together?
>
> If the strangers on the other side of the world, our children, partners, lovers, friends, and colleagues could all gather together ...could we lean on each other, learn from each other, and move forward together? What could we ... what would we do?

G o n g g g ...

I am silent. The room is silent, too. It is one of those moments when an entire gathering becomes completely still, almost suspended in time. Everyone is together, all consciousness drawn into the moment …hovering …listening …being.

I then revealed an object I had brought with me from another culture: a Native American "talking stick." It's a ceremonial piece made for this purpose, tied closely to storytelling. It's visually stimulating, adorned with traditional symbols: fur and antlers, feathers and paint. Every nuance is rich with meaning.

I explain a few of the symbols as they have been explained to me and tell the group that I am not going to be indoctrinating them into an alternative spirituality group, but that we are going to use the stick as a symbol. The stick will be our symbol of sharing truth; truth with a little "t," not a big "T." I am looking for individual truth, the kind that comes simply from speaking honestly.

I explain that we pass the stick around and everyone has the opportunity to share. It's also okay to pass, not saying anything. And, it's okay to speak on an unrelated topic if that's what people want to share. Finally, it is okay to just hold the stick in silence.

I offer. There's a pause. I have learned that silence is often necessary for thoughtful sharing. After a bit, someone takes the stick. It's my turn to listen.

One CIO shares how the poem reminded her that she misses her parents. They died just three years before. She recalls how they each guided her in subtle and small ways, how she depended on them, and now that they're gone, she's on her own. She thought of them when I mentioned "ancestors" and she wondered what they would think of her work and what they would tell her if they were still alive.

A gentleman from a large organization known for its secrecy and close relationship to the U.S. Department of Defense next wonders aloud. "How will my organization's goals contribute to the world in which my grandchildren will grow up?" He tells of the culture of invulnerability and competitiveness within his group, and reflects on what these norms imply about core values. He ends by speculating on what contributions he can make as CIO to see his organization reach its human potential.

A consultant in the group shares some of her experiences conducting corporate interventions. She says this is one of the quickest techniques she has ever seen for engaging people in the deeper implications of work-life. She connects the experience to ancient ceremonies in cultures the world over, and wonders what treasures we have lost in our rush to be civilized.

The storytelling unfolds in a quiet and relaxed pace as people take the time to let deep thoughts surface, and to listen to each other without interruption. Soon it is time to close. There seems to be a consensus that we have only just begun to discover who is in the room, beyond the job titles, and what deeper issues concern us.

It has become apparent that by calling the whole person forward to discuss important issues we get a far more thorough perspective. Our increased rapport helped us to draw on personal experiences that are not normally available as resources in the business world.

After we break, people linger for a long time, discussing what happened and how they can apply it when they return to their organizations. People call me aside to tell me over and again, "Important qualities of our community emerged with each sharing. We got to know each other in essential and relevant ways."

What happened here? Is it a legitimate contribution? This type of community storytelling invites the whole person into the workplace conversation—tacit knowledge and all. Storytelling in a community context holds the potential to revitalize the way we do business.

The end product of this type of interaction is people working better together. Social capital—the trust, reputation and shared values that contribute to a healthy culture—is increased and fortified. The people present gained a deeper appreciation of each others' strengths and weaknesses. Their authentic participation created a platform for a higher quality of work.

---

[1] First published by Information Outlook, May 2001, as part of *Bringing Us Back to Life: Storytelling and the Modern Organization*

[2] One source is *World as Lover, World as Self* by Joanna Macy and Thich Nat Hanh, Parralax Press, 1991.

JumpStart Storytelling™
Imagine If you will…

A 2-day think-tank of business professionals coming together to address critical issues. The first session propels the retreat into a high performance event, drawing everyone together & highlighting the diversity of perspectives. They are using JumpStart Storytelling™ to lift the collective spirit and maximize the impact of their time together.

JumpStart Storytelling™ is a powerful technique for quickly engaging participants in the business at hand and accelerating productive work. Designed for groups of 10 to 100, it can be customized for as few as three and as many as 400. It takes about 60 minutes and sets the stage for high performance collaboration.

JumpStart Storytelling™ will:
1. Efficiently engage every participant in the business objectives
2. Accelerate collaboration without compromising diverse perspectives
3. Effectively introduce each person to 10-15 other participants
4. Improve learning through high quality idea exchange

The magic of JumpStart Storytelling™ occurs when participants tell and listen to each other's stories, engaging the hearts and minds of their colleagues. It is a great way to begin a business gathering, involving everyone in the room. Ideas cross-pollinate, and rapport increases. The entire meeting comes to life in a way that naturally and predictably focuses the audience's collective enthusiasm on the business at hand through the participants' personal stories.

Storytelling is part of human experience. **When people share their stories, listeners naturally focus their attention, engaging with the teller's experience.** The deliberate and effective use of storytelling establishes links between participants, and sets the stage for high performance.

To create an atmosphere of collaboration it is necessary to shift away from a "broadcast" mode in which one person speaks while everyone else listens. By activating a "beehive" in which everyone is sharing, the conversation moves off of the podium and out onto the floor. **This form of storytelling has the effect of filling the room with relevant activity and enthusiasm.**

Social networking is one of the primary reasons people attend professional gatherings. Many transactions take place in the hallways: valuable news is exchanged, services and jobs are brokered, and new members are integrated within existing communities or not.

The capacity for each person to build and develop relationships during the meeting increases as they are informally introduced to others, invited to share their stories in the context of business. **This sharing is personal, face-to-face, providing a rich interaction which significantly increases the capacity of the group for social networking.**

High quality collaboration relies on multiple, conflicting points of view coming together in a collective intelligence that honors the contribution of each perspective. Building community is often mistakenly thought of as creating an environment where everybody likes each other. People perform effectively without mutual admiration. Yet, it is critical to establish an atmosphere of collective aspiration built upon respect and the capacity for each person to contribute to the group's objectives.

JUMPSTART STORYTELLING™ TEMPLATE

Introduction
5 minutes

1st Story Table:
10 - 20 minutes

1. Each person recalls an experience around the theme of the gathering
2. Facilitator provides example of telling this in story format in 90 seconds more or less.
3. In small groups of 6-12 each person shares their story.

2nd Story Table:
5 - 15 minutes

1. New small groups are formed—all new faces.
2. Storytelling is repeated. Same story, different listeners

Clusters & Chains:
5 minutes

1. Each person recalls the story that most captured their attention.
2. Everyone stands up, finds the teller, and puts their hand on his or her shoulder.
3. Those with most hands on their shoulders (i.e., the most people have selected them) are asked to share their stories with the plenary—they become the "group storytellers."

Plenary Storytelling:
10 minutes

1. The group storytellers tell their stories. Each story is followed by 20 seconds of silence, rather than applause. Audience is encouraged to quietly notice how the story engages them.
2. Each story is explored through the listeners' perspective. The question is answered, "Why was this story selected as being important to our gathering?"

Concluding Remarks
5 minutes

Total time: 40–60 minutes

CONCLUSION

Community is the natural way that human beings work and learn together. Beehives leverage this ability, using it to benefit organizations, meetings and the people who participate.

Beehives increase individual and organizational performance. The benefits are significant: greater trust, better project execution, faster training, improved communications, stronger partnerships, improved learning and the increased value that comes from utilizing different perspectives.

Our world is taking us to new frontiers where we work and learn together at accelerated rates. Community is the natural compliment to the new technologies. It is adapting to the global village, growing along the fiber-optic skeleton of the Internet and uniting people around the globe.

Those organizations that bring people together in new ways will be the leaders of tomorrow. They will make use of the tremendous potential waiting to be awakened in our hearts and minds.

Please stay in touch with me and this work. You may join my email newsletter and learn more by visiting me on the web at www.SethKahan.com.

I wish you sweet rewards in the years to come!

Seth Kahan
Seth@SethKahan.com

Bibliography

Albrecht, Karl, **The Power of Minds at Work: Organizational Intelligence in Action,** AMACOM, 2003

Bennet, Alex, and Bennet, David, **Organizational Survival in the New World: The Intelligent Complex Adaptive System,** KMCI Press, 2004

Blackiston, Howland, **Beekeeping for Dummies,** Hungry Minds, Inc., 2002

Bohm, David, **Unfolding Meaning: A Weekend of Dialogue,** Routledge, 1985

Collison, Chris, and Parcell, Geoff, **Learning to Fly: Practical Lessons from one of the World's Leading Knowledge Companies,** Capstone Publishing Limited, 2001

Cross, Rob, and Parker, Andrew, **The Hidden Power of Social Networks: Understanding How Work Really Gets Done in Organizations,** Harvard Business School Press, 2004

Davenport, Thomas H., and Prusak, Laurence, **Working Knowledge: How Organizations Manage What They Know,** Harvard Business School Press, 1998

Davenport, Thomas H., and Prusak, Laurence, and Wilson, James H., **What's the Big Idea? Creating and Capitalizing on the Best Management Thinking,** Harvard Business School Press, 2003

de Geus, Arie, **The Living Company: Habits for Survival in a Turbulent Business Environment,** Harvard Business School Press, 1997

Denning, Stephen, **The Springboard – How Storytelling Ignites Action in Knowledge-Era Organizations,** Butterworth-Heinemann, 2000

Denning, Stephen, **Squirrel, Inc.—A Fable of Leadership through Storytelling,** Jossey-Bass, 2004

Dixon, Nancy, **Common Knowledge: How Companies Thrive by Sharing What They Know,** Harvard Business School Press, 2000

Fisher, Kimball, and Fisher, Mareen Duncan, **The Distributed Mind: Achieving High Performance Through the Collective Intelligence of Knowledge Work Teams,** AMACOM, 1998

Fulford, Robert, **The Triumph of Narrative: Storytelling in the Age of Mass Culture,** Anansi Press, 1999

Kounalakis, Markos, and Banks, Drew, and Daus, Kim, **Beyond Spin: The Power of Strategic Corporate Journalism**, Jossey-Bass, 1999

Maguire, Jack, **The Power of Personal Storytelling: Spinning Tales to Connect with Others,** Putnam Publishing Group, 1998

McKee, Robert, **Story: Substance, Structure, Style and the Principles of Screenwriting,** HarperCollins, 1997

Palmer, Parker J., **The Courage to Teach: Exploring the Inner Landscape of a Teacher's Life,** Jossey-Bass, 1998

Rumizen, Melissie Clemmons, Ph.D., **The Complete Idiot's Guide to Knowledge Management,** ALPHA, 2002

Senge, Peter, and Scharmer, C. Otto, and Jaworski, Joseph, and Flowers, Betty Sue, **Presence: Human Purpose and the Field of the Future,** the Society of Organizational Learning, 2004

Turner, Mark, **The Literary Mind,** Oxford University Press, 1996

Wenger, Etienne, and McDermott, Richard, and Snyder, William M., **Cultivating Communities of Practice: A Guide to Managing Knowledge,** Harvard Business School Press, 2000

ACKNOWLEDGEMENTS

Many contributed. At the risk of leaving some out, I would like to thank the following for their contributions. Foremost is my family, especially my wife, Laura Baron, who made valuable contributions to this book. I want to thank, too, Gabriel, George & Jon Roehm, Furman Riley, and Joe Mancini. Colleagues who have provided assistance, guidance and support along the way include:

Jane Anderson	Ellen deFilipis	Andrew Kutt	Lesley Shneier
Edita Andreis	Steve Denning	Denise Lee	Jimmy Neil Smith
Gregory Balestrero	Patti Digh	Michael Margolis	John D. Smith
Noa Baum	Nancy Dixon	Richard McDermott	Dave Snowden
Christin Berry	Mark Doherty	Chris McEntee	Scott Steen
Kris Bieg	Elizabeth Doty	Peter Midgley	Jeff Stemke
Madelyn Blair	Ken Doyle	Roger Morier	Donna Stemmer
Anne Blouin	Marie Draper	Mark Moris	Bart Stevens
Jim Brady	Larry Forster	Susan Newman	Rick Stone
Scott Briscoe	Lynne Feingold	Don Norris	Vickie Sullivan
John Seely Brown	Carina Goihman	Carla O'Dell	Erick Thompson
Michael Burtha	GoldnFleece	Ann Oliveri	Ruth Thompson
Paul Cadario	Newton Holt	Patricia Overend	Stephen Townsend
Ira Chalphin	Patricia Hord	George Por	Bob Van Hook
Rory Chase	Peter Hutchins	Todd Post	Gaddi Vasquez
Roberto Chavez	Marcia Jackson	Pauline Ramprasad	Alan Weiss
Xavier Coll	Debbie Kahn	Gerry Rice	Etienne Wenger
Paul Costello	Nasim Kassum	Rudy Ruggles	Gail S. Williams
Sharon Cox	Lisa Kimball	Melissie Rumizen	James Wolfensohn
Rob Creekmore	Kanu Kogod	Lee Salmon	
Paul Crystal	Greta Kotler	Susan Sarfati	Jan Wright
Jeff de Cagna	Michael Kull	Chuck Seeley	